DON'T EAT THE YELLOW SNOW
POP MUSIC WISDOM

EDITED AND DESIGNED BY
MARCUS KRAFT

BIS PUBLISHERS

WHEN TIMES ARE PARTICULARLY DIFFICULT, AND YOU ARE
LIKELY TO SLIP INTO DESPAIR, SOME OF THE GREATEST POP
SONGS CAN PROVIDE TRUE COMFORT AND HELP YOU TO MAKE
IT THROUGH THE PAIN.

IT ALL BEGAN WHILE I WAS TRAVELLING IN ASIA: IT HAD BEEN
RAINING CATS AND DOGS FOR A WEEK. TO KEEP MY SPIRITS UP,
I LISTENED TO MUSIC, A LOT OF MUSIC. THIS MADE ME REALISE
THAT LOTS OF SONGS GIVE GOOD ADVICE OR WORLDLY WISDOM.
HENCEFORWARD, I ASKED EVERY BACKPACKER ON MY TRIP AND EVERY
FRIEND BACK HOME IF THEY KNEW SUCH SONGS. SOON, THE
COLLECTION HAD A REMARKABLE NUMBER ...OVER 500 SONGS.

THIS BOOK IS A SELECTION OF THE BEST PIECES OF ADVICE.
A LOT OF THEM ARE SUPPOSED TO BE SERIOUS; SOME OF THEM
ARE SAID WITH A WINK; ALL OF THEM HAVE THE ABILITY TO
MAKE US VIEW SOMETHING FROM A DIFFERENT PERSPECTIVE. THE
SONGS REPRESENT THE POPULAR MUSIC STYLES FROM THE
LAST 50 YEARS, FROM ROCK TO FOLK, AND FROM PUNK TO HIP HOP

THIS BOOK LISTS 250 OF THE BEST SONGS FOR TIMES WHEN
SOLID ADVICE IS NEEDED. IT'S A COLLECTION OF FAMOUS ADVICE
SONGS, BUT THERE ARE ALSO MANY SURPRISES.

MARCUS KRAFT
ZURICH, 2012

ANYTHING IS HARD TO FIND
WHEN YOU WILL NOT OPEN YOUR EYES
WHEN WILL YOU ACCEPT YOURSELF?
– THE SMITHS

ACCEPT YOURSELF

I DON'T NEED NO LUXURIES
'LONG AS YOU ARE UNDERSTANDIN'
I'M NOT DIFFICULT TO PLEASE
ACT NICE AND GENTLE TO ME
— THE BLACK KEYS

ACT NICE AND GENTLE

THERE AIN'T NO DRINK, NO DRUG, AH TELL THEM, ANGELS
THERE'S NOTHING PURE ENOUGH TO BE A CURE FOR LOVE
— LEONARD COHEN

AIN'T NO CURE FOR LOVE

WHEN YOU'RE CHEWING ON LIFE'S GRISTLE
DON'T GRUMBLE, GIVE A WHISTLE
AND THIS'LL HELP THINGS TURN OUT FOR THE BEST
AND ALWAYS LOOK ON THE BRIGHT SIDE OF LIFE
— ERIC IDLE

ALWAYS LOOK ON THE BRIGHT SIDE OF LIFE

WHAT HAPPENS WHEN YOU LOSE EVERYTHING
YOU JUST START AGAIN
YOU START ALL OVER AGAIN
APPLY SOME PRESSURE
— MAXIMO PARK

APPLY SOME PRESSURE

GIVE UP THIS FIGHT, THERE ARE NO SECOND CHANCES
THIS TIME I MIGHT
TO ASK THE SEA FOR ANSWERS
— PLACEBO

ASK FOR ANSWERS

HE'S RETURNED TO KILL THE LIGHT
THEN WHEN HE'S FOUND WHO HE'S LOOKING FOR
LISTEN IN AWE AND YOU'LL HEAR HIM
BARK AT THE MOON
— OZZY OSBOURNE

18

BARK AT THE MOON

YOU MAY NOT HAVE A CAR AT ALL
BUT JUST REMEMBER BROTHERS AND SISTERS
YOU CAN STILL STAND TALL
JUST BE THANKFUL FOR WHAT YOU'VE GOT
— MASSIVE ATTACK

BE THANKFUL FOR WHAT YOU'VE GOT

TO BE YOURSELF IS ALL THAT YOU CAN DO
SOMEONE FINDS SALVATION IN EVERYONE
ANOTHER ONLY PAIN
— AUDIOSLAVE

BE YOURSELF

YOU WANNA STAY ALIVE
BETTER DO WHAT YOU CAN
SO BEAT IT
JUST BEAT IT
— MICHAEL JACKSON

BEAT IT

TRYING THOUGH I KNOW IT'S WRONG
BLOWING IT TO HELL AND GONE
WISHING THOUGH I NEVER COULD
BLOW UP THE UPSIDE WORLD
— SOUNDGARDEN

BLOW UP THE OUTSIDE WORLD

NO MATTER WHAT
YOU JUST CAN'T STOP
BOP 'TIL YOU DROP
— THE RAMONES

BOP 'TIL YOU DROP

I TRY TO LAUGH ABOUT IT
HIDING THE TEARS IN MY EYES
BECAUSE BOYS DON'T CRY
— THE CURE

BOYS DON'T CRY

YOU KNOW THE DAY DESTROYS THE NIGHT
NIGHT DIVIDES THE DAY
TRIED TO RUN, TRIED TO HIDE
BREAK ON THROUGH TO THE OTHER SIDE
— THE DOORS

BREAK ON THROUGH (TO THE OTHER SIDE)

BRING YOUR DAUGHTER, BRING YOUR DAUGHTER TO THE SLAUGHTER
LET HER GO, LET HER GO, LET HER GO
— IRON MAIDEN

BRING YOUR DAUGHTER TO THE SLAUGHTER

CARRY ON MY SONS FOREVER
CARRY ON WHEN I AM GONE
CARRY ON WHEN THE DAY IS LONG
FOREVER CARRY ON
FOR AS LONG AS WE'RE TOGETHER
— MANOWAR

CARRY ON

IF YOU WANT TO BE SOMEBODY ELSE
IF YOU'RE TIRED OF FIGHTING BATTLES WITH YOURSELF
IF YOU WANT TO BE SOMEBODY ELSE
CHANGE YOUR MIND
— SISTER HAZEL

CHANGE YOUR MIND

NO MATTER WHAT I DO, YOU SAY I NEVER DO IT RIGHT
PLAYIN TO WIN, STAYIN UP ALL NIGHT
ALL THOSE WITH PRIDE AND EXCELLENCE
FUCK YOU AND YOUR INTELLIGENCE
— SLAPSTICK

CHEAT TO WIN

CLEAN UP YOUR OWN BACKYARD
YOU TEND TO YOUR BUSINESS, I'LL TEND TO MINE
— ELVIS PRESLEY

CLEAN UP YOUR OWN BACKYARD

COME AS YOU ARE, AS YOU WERE
AS I WANT YOU TO BE
AS A FRIEND, AS A FRIEND
AS AN OLD ENEMY
— NIRVANA

COME AS YOU ARE

COME ON GET HIGH
SWITCH OFF GET HIGH
SO WE CAN FALL IN LOVE AGAIN
— ARCHIVE

COME
ON
GET
HIGH

ONE THING I CAN TELL YOU
IS YOU GOT TO BE FREE
COME TOGETHER
RIGHT NOW OVER ME
— THE BEATLES

COME
TOGETHER

IF YOU'RE WORRIED AND YOU CAN'T SLEEP
JUST COUNT YOUR BLESSINGS INSTEAD OF SHEEP
AND YOU'LL FALL ASLEEP
COUNTING YOUR BLESSINGS
— BING CROSBY

COUNT YOUR BLESSINGS (INSTEAD OF SHEEP)

IN THE END
(UNLESS YOU'RE READY TO LEAVE IT)
YOU JUST REPEAT YOURSELF AGAIN
(BUT YOU DON'T KNOW YOU NEED IT)
WHEN YOU DON'T KNOW WHO YOU ARE
(DO YOU REALLY BELIEVE IN IT?)
YOU DIG YOURSELF THE HOLE YOU'RE IN
— THE CHEMICAL BROTHERS

DIG YOUR OWN HOLE

WELL I'VE BEEN THINKING 'BOUT
ALL THE PLACES WE'VE SURFED AND DANCED AND
ALL THE FACES WE'VE MISSED SO LET'S GET
BACK TOGETHER AND DO IT AGAIN
— THE BEACH BOYS

DO
IT
AGAIN

DON'T YOU GIVE A FUCK ANYMORE NOW
SHE'S GIVIN' UP ON YOU NOW
DO IT FOR THE KIDS THEY SAY
IT AIN'T ABOUT YOU ANYWAY
— VELVET REVOLVER

DO IT FOR THE KIDS

DO IT THE HEART WAY
AND ITS HARD TO LOOSE
ONLY THE SOFT WAY
HAS A CHANCE OF FAILING
YOU HAVE TO CHOOSE
— THIEVERY CORPORATION

DO IT THE HEART WAY

TURN OFF YOUR RADIO. QUIT YOUR JOB
DO SOMETHING DIFFERENT. DISAPPEAR
— BRAVE COMBO

DO SOMETHING DIFFERENT

UH DON'T BE CRUEL
'CAUSE I WOULD NEVER BE THAT CRUEL TO YOU
UH NO, UH NO, UH DON'T BE CRUEL
UH GIRL, YOU NEED TO CHANGE YOUR ATTITUDE
UH NO, OH, UH DON'T BE CRUEL
— BOBBY BROWN

DON'T BE CRUEL

IF YOU ARE SHY FOR TOMORROW YOU'LL BE SHY FOR 1000 DAYS
NOW IS YOUR TIME TO SHINE
— THE LIBERTINES

DON'T BE SHY

THERE'S A HEAVEN ABOVE YOU BABY
AND DON'T YOU CRY TONIGHT
— GUNS'N'ROSES

DON'T CRY

AND SHE SAID, WITH A TEAR IN HER EYE:
"WATCH OUT WHERE THE HUSKIES GO
AND DON'T YOU EAT THAT YELLOW SNOW"
— FRANK ZAPPA

DON'T EAT THE YELLOW SNOW

DON'T LET THEM STOP YOU BELIEVING
AND DON'T LET THEM FIND YOU BREATHING
— THE ZUTONS

DON'T GET LOST IN HEAVEN
THEY GOT LOCKS ON THE GATE
DON'T GO OVER THE EDGE
YOU'LL MAKE A BIG MISTAKE
— GORILLAZ

DON'T GET LOST IN HEAVEN

```
DON'T GIVE UP
'COS YOU HAVE FRIENDS
DON'T GIVE UP
YOU'RE NOT BEATEN YET
DON'T GIVE UP
I KNOW YOU CAN MAKE IT GOOD
— PETER GABRIEL
```

DON'T GIVE UP

AH BUT DON'T GO HOME WITH YOUR HARD-ON
IT WILL ONLY DRIVE YOU INSANE
YOU CAN'T SHAKE IT (OR BREAK IT) WITH YOUR MOTOWN
YOU CAN'T MELT IT DOWN IN THE RAIN
— LEONARD COHEN

DON'T GO HOME WITH YOUR HARD-ON

IF YOU'RE COLD I'LL KEEP YOU WARM
IF YOU'RE LOW JUST HOLD ON
CAUSE I WILL BE YOUR SAFETY
OH DON'T LEAVE HOME
— DIDO

DON'T LEAVE HOME

TWO EYES TRUTH

DON'T YOU WANNA BE MORE THAN FRIENDS
HOLD ME TIGHT AND DON'T LET GO
— EN VOGUE

DON'T LET GO (LOVE)

HER SOUL SLIDES AWAY
BUT "DON'T LOOK BACK IN ANGER"
I HEARD YOU SAY
— OASIS

DON'T LOOK BACK IN ANGER

IF YOU MAKE IT TO THE TOP AND YOU WANNA STAY ALIVE
DON'T LOSE YOUR HEAD
— QUEEN

DON'T LOSE YOUR HEAD

OH ALL THAT I KNOW
THERE'S NOTHING HERE TO RUN FROM
CAUSE HERE
EVERYBODY HERE'S GOT SOMEBODY TO LEAN ON
— COLDPLAY

DON'T
PANIC

DON'T PAY THE FERRYMAN
DON'T EVEN FIX A PRICE
DON'T PAY THE FERRYMAN
UNTIL HE GETS YOU TO THE OTHER SIDE
— CHRIS DE BURGH

DON'T PAY THE FERRYMAN

SO DON'T SAY GOODBYE
DON'T TURN AWAY
IT DOESN'T HAVE TO END TODAY
— U2

DON'T SAY GOODBYE

I TELL YA IT'S AN EASY THING
WHEN IT'S YOU AND ME
BUT DON'T SHIT WHERE YOU EAT, MY FRIEND
— WEEN

DON'T SHIT WHERE YOU EAT

I'VE HEARD IT ALL A MILLION TIMES BEFORE
TAKE OFF YOUR COAT, MY LOVE, AND CLOSE THE DOOR
DON'T SLEEP IN THE SUBWAY, DARLIN'
— PETULA CLARK

DON'T SLEEP IN THE SUBWAY

INSIDE HER THERE'S LONGING
THIS GIRL'S AN OPEN PAGE
BOOK MARKING - SHE'S SO CLOSE NOW
THIS GIRL IS HALF HIS AGE
— THE POLICE

DON'T STAND SO CLOSE TO ME

WELL THE ONLY THING I ASK OF YOU
IS TO HAND ME BACK SOME PRIDE
DON'T YOU DUMP ME ON SOME DUSTY STREET
AND HANG ME OUT TO DRY
— THE ROLLING STONES

DON'T STOP

KEEP ON WITH THE FORCE DON'T STOP
DON'T STOP 'TIL YOU GET ENOUGH
— MICHAEL JACKSON

DON'T STOP 'TIL YOU GET ENOUGH

HE LAUGHED AND KISSED HIS MOM
AND SAID: "YOUR BILLY JOE'S A MAN
I CAN SHOOT AS QUICK AND STRAIGHT AS ANYBODY CAN
BUT I WOULDN'T SHOOT WITHOUT A CAUSE"
— JOHNNY CASH

DON'T TAKE YOUR GUNS TO TOWN

DON'T TALK JUST KISS
LET YOUR TONGUE FOOL AROUND
LET'S FOOL AROUND
— RIGHT SAID FRED

DON'T TALK JUST KISS

WHEN YOU WERE JUST A YOUNG
GIRL AND STILL IN SCHOOL
HOW COME YOU NEVER
LEARNED THE GOLDEN RULE?
— RICK SPRINGFIELD

DON'T TALK TO STRANGERS

WE NEVER DID TOO MUCH TALKIN' ANYWAY
SO DON'T THINK TWICE, IT'S ALL RIGHT
— BOB DYLAN

DON'T THINK TWICE, IT'S ALL RIGHT

IN EVERY LIFE WE HAVE SOME TROUBLE
WHEN YOU WORRY YOU MAKE IT DOUBLE
DON'T WORRY, BE HAPPY
— BOBBY MCFERRIN

110

DON'T WORRY, BE HAPPY

CAN YOU FEEL A LITTLE LOVE?
DREAM ON, DREAM ON
— DEPECHE MODE

DREAM ON

COME ON, JOIN HANDS
DROP THE HATE
FORGIVE EACH OTHER
— FATBOY SLIM

DROP THE HATE

DRY YOUR EYES MATE
I KNOW IT'S HARD TO TAKE BUT HER MIND HAS BEEN MADE UP
THERE'S PLENTY MORE FISH IN THE SEA
— THE STREETS

EASE YOU'RE FEET OFF IN THE SEA
MY DARLING IT'S THE PLACE TO BE
TAKE YOUR SHOES OFF CURL YOUR TOES
I WILL FRAME THIS MOMENT IN TIME
— BELLE & SEBASTIAN

EASE YOUR FEET IN THE SEA

```
EAT THE RICH
THERE'S ONLY ONE THING THEY'RE GOOD FOR
EAT THE RICH
TAKE ONE BITE NOW - COME BACK FOR MORE
— AEROSMITH
```

EAT THE RICH

ALL I EVER WANTED, ALL I EVER NEEDED
IS HERE IN MY ARMS
WORDS ARE VERY UNNECESSARY
THEY CAN ONLY DO HARM
ENJOY THE SILENCE, ENJOY THE SILENCE
ENJOY THE SILENCE
— DEPECHE MODE

ENJOY THE SILENCE

DON'T LET YOURSELF GO
EVERYBODY CRIES AND EVERYBODY HURTS SOMETIMES
— R.E.M.

EVERYBODY HURTS

EVERYBODY NEEDS SOMEBODY TO LOVE (SOMEONE TO LOVE)
SWEETHEART TO MISS (SWEETHEART TO MISS)
SUGAR TO KISS (SUGAR TO KISS)
— BLUES BROTHERS

EVERYBODY NEEDS SOMEBODY TO LOVE

EVERYBODY WANTS TO RULE THE WORLD
SAY THAT YOU'LL NEVER NEVER NEVER NEVER NEED IT
— TEARS FOR FEARS

EVERYBODY WANTS TO RULE THE WORLD

IF I COULD OFFER YOU ONLY ONE TIP FOR THE FUTURE
SUNSCREEN WOULD BE IT. THE LONG TERM BENEFITS
OF SUNSCREEN HAVE BEEN PROVED BY SCIENTISTS WHEREAS
THE REST OF MY ADVICE HAS NO BASIS MORE RELIABLE
THAN MY OWN MEANDERING
— BAZ LUHRMAN

EVERYBODY'S FREE (TO WEAR SUNSCREEN)

CHANGE YOUR HEART
LOOK AROUND YOU
CHANGE YOUR HEART
IT WILL ASTOUND YOU
I NEED YOU LOVIN'
LIKE THE SUNSHINE
EVERYBODY'S GOT TO LEARN SOMETIME
— BECK

EVERYBODY'S GOTTA LEARN SOMETIMES

EVERYDAY IS A WINDING ROAD
I GET A LITTLE BIT CLOSER
EVERYDAY IS A FADED SIGN
I GET A LITTLE BIT CLOSER TO FEELING FINE
— SHERYL CROW

EVERYDAY IS A WINDING ROAD

EVERYTHING IS EVERYTHING
WHAT IS MEANT TO BE, WILL BE
AFTER WINTER, MUST COME SPRING
CHANGE, IT COMES EVENTUALLY
— LAURYN HILL

EVERYTHING IS EVERYTHING

SO IF YOU WANT IT RIGHT NOW, MAKE HIM SHOW YOU HOW
EXPRESS WHAT HE'S GOT, OH BABY READY OR NOT
— MADONNA

EXPRESS YOURSELF

YOU CAN'T TOUCH IT SEE IT BREATHE IT
FEEL - IT'S ALL YOU CAN
— STEREOPHONICS

FEEL

MAN, LIVING AT HOME IS SUCH A DRAG
NOW YOUR MOM THREW AWAY YOUR BEST PORNO MAG (BUSTED!)
YOU GOTTA FIGHT FOR YOUR RIGHT TO PARTY
— BEASTIE BOYS

FIGHT FOR YOUR RIGHT

FIND YOURSELF ANOTHER GIRL
WHO WILL LOVE YOU TRUE TRUE TRUE
FIND YOURSELF ANOTHER GIRL
SAVE ALL HER LOVE AND KISSES JUST FOR YOU
— THE HIVES

FIND ANOTHER GIRL

LET'S FADE INTO THE SUN
LET YOUR SPIRIT FLY
WHERE WE ARE ONE
JUST FOR A LITTLE FUN
— LENNY KRAVITZ

FLY AWAY

BEFORE YOU CAN READ ME YOU GOT TO
LEARN HOW TO SEE ME, I SAID
FREE YOUR MIND AND THE REST WILL FOLLOW
BE COLOR BLIND, DON'T BE SO SHALLOW
— EN VOGUE

YOU DON'T ALWAYS HAVE TO FUCK HER HARD
IN FACT SOMETIMES THAT'S NOT RIGHT TO DO
SOMETIMES YOU'VE GOT TO MAKE SOME LOVE
AND FUCKING GIVE HER SOME SMOOCHES TOO
— TENACIOUS D

WAR!
FUCK THE SYSTEM!
WAR!
FUCK THE SYSTEM!
— SYSTEM OF A DOWN

GET A HAIRCUT AND GET A REAL JOB
CLEAN YOUR ACT UP AND DON'T BE A SLOB
— GEORGE THOROGOOD

GET A HAIRCUT

GO HOME
GET BACK, GET BACK
BACK TO WHERE YOU ONCE BELONGED
— THE BEATLES

GET
BACK

GOT TO GET BEHIND THE MULE
IN THE MORNING AND PLOW
— TOM WAITS

HOW YOU GONNA DO IT IF YOU REALLY DON'T WANT DO DANCE
BY STANDING ON THE WALL?
GET YOUR BACK UP OFF THE WALL
— KOOL AND THE GANG

GET DOWN ON IT

YOU CAN REACH ME BY CARAVAN
CROSS THE DESERT LIKE AN ARAB MAN
I DON'T CARE HOW YOU GET HERE
JUST - GET HERE IF YOU CAN
— OLETA ADAMS

GET
HERE

GET INTO THE GROOVE
BOY YOU'VE GOT TO PROVE
YOUR LOVE TO ME, YEAH
— MADONNA

164

GET INTO THE GROOVE

GET IT TOGETHER
YOU WANNA HEAL YOUR BODY
YOU HAVE TO HEAL YOUR HEART
WHATSOEVER YOU SOW YOU WILL REAP
GET IT TOGETHER
— INDIA ARI

GET IT TOGETHER

```
I SAID HOLD ON TO SOMEBODY
WHEN YOU GET A LITTLE LONELY, DEAR
HEY HEY, HOLD ON TO THAT MAN'S HEART
YEAH, GET IT, WANT IT, HOLD IT, NEED IT
GET IT, WANT IT, NEED IT, HOLD IT
GET IT WHILE YOU CAN, YEAH
— JANIS JOPLIN
```

GET OFF THE INTERNET!
I'LL MEET YOU IN THE STREET
— LE TIGRE

GET OFF THE INTERNET

WHAT IF I HAVE FORGOTTEN HOW?
CUT MY LOSSES AND GET OUT NOW
GET OUT, RIGHT NOW!
— FAITH NO MORE

GET OUT

C'MON PEOPLE NOW,
SMILE ON YOUR BROTHER
EV'RYBODY GET TOGETHER
TRY AND LOVE ONE ANOTHER RIGHT NOW
— THE YOUNGBLOODS

GET TOGETHER

GET UP, STAND UP, STAND UP FOR YOUR RIGHTS
GET UP, STAND UP, DON'T GIVE UP THE FIGHT
— BOB MARLEY

GET UP, STAND UP

GIRLS ARE OUT TO GET YOU
ONE BIRD IN THE HAND IS BETTER
THAN TWO IN THE BUSH, SO THEY SAY
— THE FASCINATIONS

GIRLS ARE OUT TO GET YOU

SOME BOYS TAKE A BEAUTIFUL GIRL
AND HIDE HER AWAY FROM THE REST OF THE WORLD
I WANT TO BE THE ONE TO WALK IN THE SUN
OH GIRLS THEY WANT TO HAVE FUN
— CYNDI LAUPER

GIRLS JUST WANT TO HAVE FUN

GIVE A LITTLE BIT
GIVE A LITTLE BIT OF YOUR LOVE TO ME
— SUPERTRAMP

GIVE A LITTLE BIT

GIVE IT AWAY, GIVE IT AWAY, GIVE IT AWAY, NOW
I CAN'T TELL IF I'M A KING PIN OR A PAUPER
— RED HOT CHILI PEPPERS

GIVE IT AWAY

EV'RYBODY'S TALKING ABOUT
BAGISM, SHAGISM, DRAGISM, MADISM, RAGISM, TAGISM
THIS-ISM, THAT-ISM, IS-M, IS-M, IS-M
ALL WE ARE SAYING IS GIVE PEACE A CHANCE
— JOHN LENNON

GIVE PEACE A CHANCE

(GO WEST) LIFE IS PEACEFUL THERE
(GO WEST) IN THE OPEN AIR
(GO WEST) WHERE THE SKIES ARE BLUE
(GO WEST) THIS IS WHAT WE'RE GONNA DO
— PET SHOP BOYS

GO
WEST

I CAN GO WITH THE FLOW
DO YOU BELIEVE IT IN YOUR HEAD?
— QUEENS OF THE STONE AGE

GO WITH THE FLOW

YOU CAN GO YOUR OWN WAY
GO YOUR OWN WAY
YOU CAN CALL IT
ANOTHER LONELY DAY
— FLEETWOOD MAC

GO YOUR OWN WAY

GOD GAVE ROCK AND ROLL TO YOU
GAVE ROCK AND ROLL TO YOU
PUT IT IN THE SOUL OF EVERYONE
— KISS

GOD GAVE ROCK'N'ROLL TO YOU

IT MAY BE THE DEVIL OR IT MAY BE THE LORD
BUT YOU'RE GONNA HAVE TO SERVE SOMEBODY
— BOB DYLAN

GOTTA SERVE SOMEBODY

GUARD YOUR GRILL, KNUCKLE UP
I AIN'T THE TYPE TO GIVE UP
GUARD YOUR GRILL, KNUCKLE UP
I SMOKE FIRST, SO WHAT'S UP?
— NAUGHTY BY NATURE

GUARD YOUR GRILL

YOU HAVE FOUND ANOTHER
OH BABY I MUST GO AWAY
SO HANG DOWN YOUR HEAD FOR SORROW
HANG DOWN YOUR HEAD FOR ME
— TOM WAITS

HANG DOWN YOUR HEAD

```
COME IN HERE, DEAR BOY, HAVE A CIGAR
YOU'RE GONNA GO FAR, FLY HIGH
YOU'RE NEVER GONNA DIE
YOU'RE GONNA MAKE IT IF YOU TRY
— PINK FLOYD
```

HAVE A CIGAR

HOLD THE LINE
LOVE ISN'T ALWAYS ON TIME
— TOTO

HOLD THE LINE

HONOUR YOUR MOTHER AND YOUR FATHER
THAT YOUR DAYS MAY BE LONG ON THE LAND
CHILDREN, OBEY YOUR PARENTS AND THE LAW
THIS IS THE LAW OF THE PROPHETS
— DESMOND DEKKER

HONOUR YOUR MOTHER AND FATHER

NOTHING THAT'S FORCED CAN EVER BE RIGHT
IF IT DOESN'T COME NATURALLY, LEAVE IT
THAT'S WHAT SHE SAID AS SHE TURNED OUT THE LIGHT
AND WE BENT OUR BACKS AS SLAVES OF THE NIGHT
— AL STEWART

IF IT DOESN'T COME NATURALLY, LEAVE IT

FOREVER CONDITIONED TO BELIEVE THAT WE CAN'T LIVE
WE CAN'T LIVE HERE AND BE HAPPY WITH LESS
SO MANY RICHES, SO MANY SOULS
EVERYTHING WE SEE WE WANT TO POSSESS
— STING

IF YOU LOVE SOMEBODY SET THEM FREE

A PRETTY WOMAN MAKES HER HUSBAND LOOK SMALL
AND VERY OFTEN CAUSES HIS DOWNFALL
AS SOON AS HE MARRIES HER
THEN SHE STARTS TO DO
THE THINGS THAT WILL BREAK HIS HEART
— JIMMY SOUL

IF YOU
WANT TO
BE HAPPY
(GET AN
UGLY GIRL
TO MARRY
YOU)

WHEN YOU GET KNOCKED DOWN YOU GOTTA GET BACK UP
I AIN'T THE SHARPEST KNIFE IN THE DRAWER
BUT I KNOW ENOUGH, TO KNOW
IF YOUR GONNA BE DUMB, YOU GOTTA BE TOUGH
— ROGER ALAN WADE

IMAGINE NO POSSESSIONS
I WONDER IF YOU CAN
NO NEED FOR GREED OR HUNGER
A BROTHERHOOD OF MAN
— JOHN LENNON

IMAGINE

SO MANY TEARS I'VE CRIED
SO MUCH PAIN INSIDE
BUT BABY IT AIN'T OVER 'TIL IT'S OVER
SO MANY YEARS WE'VE TRIED
— LENNY KRAVITZ

IT AIN'T OVER 'TIL IT'S OVER

```
IT MAKES NO DIFFERENCE
IF IT'S SWEET OR HOT
JUST GIVE THAT RHYTHM
EVERYTHING YOU'VE GOT
IT DON'T MEAN A THING
IF IT AIN'T GOT THAT SWING
— DUKE ELLINGTON
```

IT DON'T MEAN A THING (IF IT AIN'T GOT THAT SWING)

WELL, I WANNA BE YOUR LOVER, BABY
I DON'T WANNA BE YOUR BOSS
DON'T SAY I NEVER WARNED YOU
WHEN YOUR TRAIN GETS LOST
— BOB DYLAN

IT TAKES
A LOT TO
LAUGH,
IT TAKES
A TRAIN
TO CRY

OH LORD IT'S HARD TO BE HUMBLE
WHEN YOU'RE PERFECT IN EVERY WAY
— MAC DAVIS

IT'S HARD TO BE HUMBLE

DON'T TELL ME THAT I'M CRAZY
DON'T TELL ME I'M NOWHERE
TAKE IT FROM ME
IT'S HIP TO BE SQUARE
— HUEY LEWIS & THE NEWS

IT'S NOW OR NEVER
COME HOLD ME TIGHT
KISS ME MY DARLING
BE MINE TONIGHT
— ELVIS PRESLEY

GO AHEAD AND JUMP
GET IT IN, JUMP
(JUMP)
GO AHEAD AND JUMP
— VAN HALEN

JUMP

BABY, BABY IT LOOKS LIKE IT'S GONNA HAIL
YOU BETTER COME INSIDE
LET ME TEACH YOU HOW TO JIVE AN' WAIL
— LOUIS PRIMA

JUMP JIVE AND WAIL

STAY WITH ME
LET'S JUST BREATHE
— PEARL JAM

JUST BREATHE

SAY THIS IS IT
DON'T SAY MAYBE
DON'T SAY NO
SAY THIS IS IT
— THE CURE

JUST SAY YES

```
KEEP ON RUNNIN'
RUNNIN' FROM MY ARMS
ONE FINE DAY I'M GONNA BE THE ONE
TO MAKE YOU UNDERSTAND
— SPENCER DAVIS GROUP
```

WHY WON'T YOU TALK TO ME
YOU NEVER TALK TO ME
WHAT ARE YOU THINKING
WHAT ARE YOU FEELING
— PINK FLOYD

KEEP TALKING

KEEP THE FAITH
DON'T LET LOVE TURN TO HATE
KEEP THE FAITH
YOU KNOW YOU'RE GONNA LIVE THROUGH THE RAIN
KEEP THE FAITH
THOUGH YOU KNOW IT'S NEVER TOO LATE
— BON JOVI

AND UHH, I KNOW THEY LIKE TO BEAT YA DOWN A LOT
WHEN YOU COME AROUND THE BLOCK, BROTHAS CLOWN A LOT
BUT PLEASE DON'T CRY, DRY YOUR EYES, NEVER LET UP
FORGIVE BUT DON'T FORGET, GIRL, KEEP YA HEAD UP
— TUPAC SHAKUR

KEEP YA HEAD UP

I SAID HONEY I'LL LIVE WITH YOU FOR THE REST OF MY LIFE
SHE SAID NO HUGGIN NO KISSIN UNTIL YOU MAKE ME YOUR WIFE
MY HONEY MY BABY DON'T PUT MY LOVE ON NO SHELF
SHE DON'T HAND ME NO LINES AND KEEP YOUR HANDS TO YOURSELF
— GEORGIA SATELLITES

KEEP YOUR HANDS TO YOURSELF

FIST IN YA FACE, IN THE PLACE
AND I'LL DROP THE STYLE CLEARLY
KNOW YOUR ENEMY ... KNOW YOUR ENEMY!
— RAGE AGAINST THE MACHINE

KNOW YOUR ENEMY

THIS IS A PUBLIC SERVICE ANNOUNCEMENT
WITH GUITAR
KNOW YOUR RIGHTS ALL THREE OF THEM
— THE CLASH

KNOW YOUR RIGHTS

I'M LOOKING FOR A COMPLICATION
LOOKING CAUSE I'M TIRED OF TRYING
MAKE MY WAY BACK HOME WHEN I LEARN TO FLY HIGH
— FOO FIGHTERS

LEARN TO FLY

WHEN I FIND MYSELF IN TIMES OF TROUBLE
MOTHER MARY COMES TO ME
SPEAKING WORDS OF WISDOM, LET IT BE
— THE BEATLES

LET IT BE

THE SADDEST PART OF A BROKEN HEART
ISN'T THE ENDING SO MUCH AS THE START
— FEIST

LET IT DIE

LET IT GO BEFORE IT KILLS YOU
LET IT FALL AND THE FADE AWAY
LET'S HAVE FUN AND DO WHAT THRILLS YOU
PLEASE DON'T WASTE ANOTHER DAY
— MORCHEEBA

LET IT GO

ROCK-A-BYE BABY
IF YOU WANNA DANCE
GRAB YOURSELF A BODY
AND TAKE A CHANCE
— AEROSMITH

LET THE MUSIC DO THE TALKING

LET THE MUSIC PLAY ON
JUST UNTIL I FEEL THIS MISERY IS GONE
MOVIN', KICKIN', GROOVIN', KEEP THE MUSIC STRONG
— BARRY WHITE

LET THE MUSIC PLAY

WHEN YOU FEEL LIKE EVERYTHING'S CHEATED
AND YOUR FRIENDS ARE TURNING BACKS UPON YOU
JUST OPEN UP YOUR HEART
AND LET IT SHINE IN
— THE 5TH DIMENSION

LET THE SUNSHINE IN

LET THERE BE LOVE
IT HEALS AND IT HURTS
SHE LEADS YOU TO HEAVEN'S DOOR
AND LEAVES YOU FOR DIRT
— SIMPLE MINDS

LET THERE BE LOVE

AND THE COMPASS SPINS
THE COMPASS SPINS BETWEEN HEAVEN AND HELL
LET YOUR SOUL BE YOUR PILOT
— STING

LET YOUR SOUL BE YOUR PILOT

WHEN TIMES ARE HARD
WHEN YOU START FEELIN' LOW
LET YOURSELF GO
WHEN THE RIVER'S RISIN' AND THE WORLD FEELS COLD
— TOM PETTY & THE HEARTBREAKERS

LET YOURSELF GO

LET'S DANCE FOR FEAR
YOUR GRACE SHOULD FALL
LET'S DANCE FOR FEAR TONIGHT IS ALL
— DAVID BOWIE

LET'S DANCE

WHEN YOU TURN AND WALK AWAY
DON'T LOOK BACK
I WANNA REMEMBER YOU, JUST LIKE THIS
LET'S JUST KISS AND SAY GOODBYE
— BARRY WHITE

LET'S

JUST

KISS

AND SAY

GOODBYE

LET'S ROCK, LET'S ROLL
THE PARTY'S ON, WE'RE HAVING A BALL
WE'RE GONNA LEAVE A STING IN YOUR SOUL
WE PUT THE ROCK BACK IN THE ROLL
— SCORPIONS

LET'S ROCK

LET'S SPEND THE NIGHT TOGETHER
DON'T HANG ME UP AND DON'T LET ME DOWN
(DON'T LET ME DOWN)
WE COULD HAVE FUN JUST GROOVIN' AROUND,
AROUND AND AROUND
— THE ROLLING STONES

AND NOW THE MARRIAGE VOW IS VERY SACRED
THE MAN HAS PUT US TOGETHER NOW
YOU OUGHT TO MAKE IT STICK TOGETHER
COME ON, COME ON, LET'S STICK TOGETHER
YOU KNOW WE MADE A VOW NOT TO LEAVE ONE ANOTHER NEVER
— BRYAN FERRY

LET'S STICK TOGETHER

YOU CAN BE ALL YOU WANT DEAR
DON'T FORGET YOUR RIOT GEAR
MAY THE WIND BLOW BEHIND YOU
MAY HAPPINESS SOMEDAY FIND YOU
— WHITE HASSLE

LIFE IS STILL SWEET

```
BABY, LIFE'S WHAT YOU MAKE IT
CAN'T ESCAPE IT
BABY, YESTERDAY'S FAVOURITE
DON'T YOU HATE IT?
— TALK TALK
```

LIFE'S WHAT YOU MAKE IT

I WANNA LIVE ALONE
I COULD BE HAPPY ON MY OWN
REST OF MY LIFE
WITH THE VAGUEST OF FEELING
— FRANZ FERDINAND

LIVE ALONE

I THINK YOU'RE THE SAME AS ME
WE SEE THINGS THEY'LL NEVER SEE
YOU AND I ARE GONNA LIVE FOREVER
WE'RE GONNA LIVE FOREVER
— OASIS

WHEN YOU WERE YOUNG AND YOUR HEART WAS AN OPEN BOOK
YOU USED TO SAY LIVE AND LET LIVE
— PAUL MCCARTNEY & WINGS

LIVE AND LET DIE

YOU GOTTA LOOK SHARP
AND YOU GOTTA HAVE NO ILLUSIONS
JUST KEEP GOING YOUR WAY LOOKING OVER YOUR SHOULDER
— JOE JACKSON

LOOK SHARP!

YOU BETTER LOSE YOURSELF IN THE MUSIC
THE MOMENT, YOU OWN IT, YOU BETTER NEVER LET IT GO
— EMINEM

LOSE YOURSELF

YOU COME ON STRONG
TOO MUCH TOO SOON
AND UNFORTUNATELY
I'M NOT AMUSED
— GOSSIP

LOVE AND LET LOVE

LOVE IS LIKE A CLOUD
HOLDS A LOT OF RAIN
LOVE HURTS, OH, LOVE HURTS
— NAZARETH

LOVE HURTS

WE ARE STRONG
NO ONE CAN TELL US WE'RE WRONG
SEARCHING OUR HEARTS FOR SO LONG
BOTH OF US KNOWING
LOVE IS A BATTLEFIELD
— PAT BENATAR

LOVE IS A BATTLEFIELD

LOVE IS A STRANGER IN AN OPEN CAR
TO TEMPT YOU IN AND DRIVE YOU FAR AWAY
— EURYTHMICS

LOVE IS A STRANGER

LOVE IS LIKE OXYGEN
YOU GET TOO MUCH, YOU GET TOO HIGH
NOT ENOUGH AND YOU'RE GONNA DIE
LOVE GETS YOU HIGH
— SWEET

LOVE IS LIKE OXYGEN

TURN YOUR HEARTACHE RIGHT INTO JOY
SHE'S A GIRL, YOU'RE A BOY
GET IT TOGETHER MAKE IT NICE
YOU AIN'T GONNA NEED ANYMORE ADVICE
— STEPHEN STILLS

LOVE THE ONE YOU'RE WITH

DON'T LET 'EM PICK GUITARS AND DRIVE THEM OLD TRUCKS
MAKE 'EM BE DOCTORS AND LAWYERS AND SUCH
— WILLIE NELSON

MAMAS DON'T LET YOUR BABIES GROW UP TO BE COWBOYS

WELL, YOU'VE LAUNDERED AND ROBBED
EVERYTHING UNDER THE SUN
AND YOUR TIME HAS NOW COME TO RUN, RUN, RUN
MONEY WON'T SAVE YOU, NO, NO
ONLY TRUTH AND RIGHT JUSTICE CAN
— JIMMY CLIFF

WATCH OUT, HE'S GONNA BREAK YOUR HEART
TRY TO UNDERSTAND
NEVER WEAR MASCARA
WHEN YOU LOVE A MARRIED MAN
– THE HANK WANGFORD BAND

NEVER
WEAR
MASCARA
(WHEN YOU
LOVE A
MARRIED
MAN)

LITTLE DARLIN' DON'T SHED NO TEARS
NO WOMAN, NO CRY
— BOB MARLEY

NOTHING IS EASY
THOUGH TIME GETS YOU WORRYING
MY FRIEND, IT'S O.K.
JUST TAKE YOUR LIFE EASY
AND STOP ALL THAT HURRYING
BE HAPPY MY WAY
— JETRHO TULL

NOTHING IS EASY

SO TO THOSE WHO WANNA RAP, I'M PERTAININ' TO YOU
BEFORE YOU PICK UP A MIC, YOU GOTTA PAY DUES, WORD
— SNOOP DOGG

PAY YA DUES

YOU SAY THERE'S A LESSON THAT YOU WANT TO TEACH
WELL HERE I AM BABY, PRACTICE WHAT YOU PREACH
— BARRY WHITE

PRACTICE WHAT YOU PREACH

FIRST THINGS FIRST MAN YOU'RE FUCKING WITH THE WORST
I'LL BE STICKING PINS IN YOUR HEAD LIKE A FUCKING NURSE
— WU-TANG CLAN

PROTECT YA NECK

COOLIN' BY DAY THEN AT NIGHT WORKING UP A SWEAT
C'MON GIRLS, LET'S GO SHOW THE GUYS THAT WE KNOW
HOW TO BECOME NUMBER ONE IN A HOT PARTY SHOW
NOW PUSH IT
— SALT'N'PEPPA

PUSH IT

HEY NOW, ALL YOU SINNERS
PUT YOUR LIGHTS ON, PUT YOUR LIGHTS ON
HEY NOW, ALL YOU CHILDREN
LEAVE YOUR LIGHTS ON, YOU BETTER LEAVE YOUR LIGHTS ON
— SANTANA (FEAT. EVERLAST)

PUT YOUR LIGHTS ON

QUE SERA, SERA
WHATEVER WILL BE, WILL BE
THE FUTURE'S NOT OURS TO SEE
QUE SERA, SERA
WHAT WILL BE, WILL BE
— DORIS DAY

QUE SERA, SERA (WHATEVER WILL BE, WILL BE)

REACH OUT AND TOUCH
SOMEBODY'S HAND
MAKE THIS WORLD A BETTER PLACE
IF YOU CAN
— DIANA ROSS

REACH
OUT
AND
TOUCH

IT IS THE NIGHT
MY BODY'S WEAK
I'M ON THE RUN
NO TIME FOR SLEEP
I'VE GOT TO RIDE
RIDE LIKE THE WIND
TO BE FREE AGAIN
— CHRISTOPHER CROSS

RIDE LIKE THE WIND

SAIL AWAY, YOU CAN FLY
ON THIS WINGS OF FREEDOM
YOU CAN REACH THE SKY
— HANS HARTZ

SAIL AWAY

CONTROL YOURSELF, LOVE IS ALL YOU NEED
CONTROL YOURSELF, OPEN UP YOUR HEART
SANCTIFY YOURSELF, SET YOURSELF FREE
— SIMPLE MINDS

SANCTIFY YOURSELF

STAY ALL NIGHT
WE'LL SAVE THE POPULATION
— RED HOT CHILI PEPPERS

338

I DON'T WANNA HEAR YOU MIGHT
THERE'S A FIRE GETTIN' NEAR AND SPARKS IGNITE
IF YOU'RE READY FOR A WILD RIDE
LET ME HEAR YOU SAY YEAH
— KISS

SAY

YEAH

EVERYBODY, GET ON THE FLOOR AND LET'S DANCE
DON'T FIGHT YOUR FEELINGS, GIVE YOURSELF A CHANCE
SHAKE SHAKE SHAKE, SHAKE SHAKE SHAKE
— KC & THE SUNSHINE BAND

SHAKE YOUR BOOTY

BEFORE YOU ASK SOME GIRL FOR HER HAND NOW (MY SON)
KEEP YOUR FREEDOM FOR AS LONG AS YOU CAN NOW
MY MAMA TOLD ME... YOU BETTER SHOP AROUND
- SMOKEY ROBINSON AND THE MIRACLES

344

SHOP AROUND

I BURN A FIRE TO STAY COOL
I BURN MYSELF
I AM THE FUEL
I NEVER MEANT TO BE CRUEL
— FUGAZI

SHUT THE DOOR

"SHUT THE FUCK UP" SHE SAID
I'M GOING FUCKING DEAF
YOU'RE ALWAYS TOO LOUD
EVERYTHING'S TOO LOUD
— BLINK 182

SHUT UP

WHEN YOU FEEL DOWN AND OUT
SING A SONG, IT'LL MAKE YOUR DAY
HERE'S A TIME TO SHOUT
SING A SONG, IT'LL MAKE A WAY
— EARTH, WIND AND FIRE

SING A SONG

SING IT BACK
BRING IT BACK
SING IT BACK TO ME
— MOLOKO

SING IT BACK

SAVE SOME FACE, YOU KNOW YOU'VE ONLY GOT ONE
CHANGE YOUR WAYS WHILE YOU'RE YOUNG
BOY, ONE DAY YOU'LL BE A MAN
OH GIRL, HE'LL HELP YOU UNDERSTAND
— THE KILLERS

SMILE
LIKE
YOU
MEAN
IT

LISTEN TO ME NOW
I NEED TO LET YOU KNOW
YOU DON'T HAVE TO GO IT ALONE
— U2

SOMETIMES YOU CAN'T MAKE IT ON YOUR OWN

I WANNA SHOOT SPEEDBALLS
BANG MY HEAD AGAINST THE WALLS
I WANNA SNIFF GLUE
'COS I CAN'T GET OVER YOU
HOW AM I GONNA SORT IT OUT?
— CEASARS

SORT IT OUT

SPEAK LOW WHEN YOU SPEAK, LOVE
OUR MOMENT IS SWIFT, LIKE SHIPS ADRIFT
WE'RE SWEPT APART, TOO SOON
— THE YOUNG GODS

SPREAD YOUR LOVE LIKE A FEVER
AND DON'T YOU EVER COME DOWN
— BLACK REBEL MOTORCYCLE CLUB

SPREAD YOUR LOVE

STAND BY YOUR MAN
GIVE HIM TWO ARMS TO CLING TO
AND SOMETHING WARM TO COME TO
WHEN NIGHTS ARE COLD AND LONELY
— TAMMY WYNETTE

STAND

BY

YOUR

MAN

BETTER STAPLE IT TOGETHER
AND CALL IT BAD WEATHER
— JACK JOHNSON

STAPLE IT TOGETHER

AND IF YOU'RE IN THE CROWN TONIGHT
HAVE A DRINK ON ME
BUT GO EASY ... STEP LIGHTLY ... STAY FREE
— THE CLASH

STAY FREE

'CAUSE ALL OF THE STARS
ARE FADING AWAY
JUST TRY NOT TO WORRY
YOU'LL SEE THEM SOME DAY
— OASIS

STOP
CRYING
YOUR
HEART
OUT

STOP! IN THE NAME OF LOVE
BEFORE YOU BREAK MY HEART
— THE SUPREMES

STOP! IN THE NAME OF LOVE

GO REAL SLOW
YOU'LL LIKE IT MORE AND MORE
TAKE IT AS IT COMES
SPECIALIZE IN HAVING FUN
— THE RAMONES

TAKE IT AS IT COMES

LEAVE ME ALONE
I'M IN CONTROL
I'M IN CONTROL
AND GIRLS LIE TOO MUCH
AND BOYS ACT TOO TOUGH
ENOUGH IS ENOUGH
— THE STROKES

TAKE IT OR LEAVE IT

IGNORANCE HAS TAKEN OVER
WE GOTTA TAKE THE POWER BACK!
— RAGE AGAINST THE MACHINE

TAKE THE POWER BACK

STEALING KISSES IN THE DARK IS JUST IMMENSE
WHERE CAN YOU GET HALF AS MUCH FOR SIXTY CENTS?
SO TAKE YOUR GIRLIE TO THE MOVIES
IF YOU CAN'T MAKE LOVE AT HOME
— DEAN MARTIN

TAKE YOUR GIRLIE TO THE MOVIES (IF YOU CAN'T MAKE LOVE AT HOME)

IT DOESN'T MATTER JUST WHO YOU ARE
OR WHERE YOU'RE GOING OR BEEN
OPEN YOUR EYES AND LOOK INTO YOUR HEART
— ERIC CLAPTON

TELL THE TRUTH

EVERYTHING IS AN ACT, EVERY LINE IS A TEST
YOUR CLOTHES ARE JUST A COSTUME
THE BEAUTY YOU KEEP IS NOT FROM WITHIN
— KATHRYN WILLIAMS

TELL THE TRUTH AS IF IT WERE LIES

THE BEST IS YET TO COME
AND WON'T THAT BE FINE
YOU THINK YOU'VE SEEN THE SUN
BUT YOU AIN'T SEEN IT SHINE
— FRANK SINATRA

THE BEST IS YET TO COME

NOW THE DRUGS DON'T WORK
THEY JUST MAKE YOU WORSE
BUT I KNOW I'LL SEE YOUR FACE AGAIN
— THE VERVE

THE FIRST CUT IS THE DEEPEST
'CAUSE WHEN IT COMES TO BEING LUCKY SHE'S CURSED
WHEN IT COMES TO LOVIN' ME SHE'S WORST
BUT WHEN IT COMES TO BEING LOVED SHE'S FIRST
THAT'S HOW I KNOW
— CAT STEVENS

THE FIRST CUT IS THE DEEPEST

FROM THE STREETS TO THE MOUNTAINS TO THE HEAVENS ABOVE
TELL EVERYBODY
TELL EVERYBODY WHAT YOU'RE DREAMING OF
TELL THEM LOVE IS THE MESSAGE AND THE MESSAGE IS LOVE
— AL GREEN

THE MESSAGE IS LOVE

```
THE SHOW MUST GO ON
INSIDE MY HEART IS BREAKING
MY MAKE-UP MAY BE FLAKING
BUT MY SMILE STILL STAYS ON
— QUEEN
```

THE SHOW MUST GO ON

GIVE UP YOURSELF UNTO THE MOMENT
THE TIME IS NOW
GIVE UP YOURSELF UNTO THE MOMENT
LET'S MAKE THIS MOMENT LAST
— MOLOKO

THE TIME IS NOW

AND LATELY I'M NOT THE ONLY ONE
I SAY NEVER TRUST ANYONE
— GARBAGE

THE TRICK IS TO KEEP BREATHING

THE WINNER TAKES IT ALL
THE LOSER'S STANDING SMALL
BESIDE THE VICTORY
THAT'S A DESTINY
— ABBA

THE WINNER TAKES IT ALL

COME ON GIRL
LET'S SNEAK OUT OF THIS PARTY
IT'S GETTING BORING
THERE'S MORE TO LIFE THAN THIS
— BJÖRK

THERE'S MORE TO LIFE THAN THIS

YEAH, THINK (THINK, THINK)
LET YOUR MIND GO, LET YOURSELF BE FREE
— ARETHA FRANKLIN

THINK

```
THINK IT OVER AND LET ME KNOW
THINK IT OVER BUT DON'T BE SLOW
— BUDDY HOLLY
```

THINK IT OVER

YOU'RE WALKIN' ALONG THE STREET, OR YOU'RE AT A PARTY
OR ELSE YOU'RE ALONE AND THEN YOU SUDDENLY DIG
YOU'RE LOOKING' IN SOMEONE'S EYES, YOU SUDDENLY REALIZE
THAT THIS COULD BE THE START OF SOMETHING BIG
— ELLA FITZGERALD

THIS COULD BE THE START OF SOMETHING BIG

I HEARD SOME KIDS TELLING ME
HOW THEY'VE LOST ALL THE FAITH IN THE WAY
THEY'VE BEEN TALKING WORLD PEACE
AND THE WAR'S IN THE STREETS
— MÖTLEY CRÜE

TIME FOR A CHANGE

TIME PASSES SLOWLY UP HERE IN THE DAYLIGHT
WE STARE STRAIGHT AHEAD AND TRY SO HARD TO STAY RIGHT
LIKE THE RED ROSE OF SUMMER THAT BLOOMS IN THE DAY
TIME PASSES SLOWLY AND FADES AWAY
— BOB DYLAN

TIME PASSES SLOWLY

I'LL PAY
WHEN TOMORROW
TOMORROW COMES TODAY
— GORILLAZ

TOMORROW COMES TODAY

TOO MUCH LOVE WILL KILL YOU
IF YOU CAN'T MAKE UP YOUR MIND
TORN BETWEEN THE LOVER
AND THE LOVE YOU LEAVE BEHIND
— QUEEN

TOO MUCH LOVE WILL KILL YOU

WHO CAN YOU TRUST
ONLY TIME REVEALS
TOSS IT UP!
— TUPAC SHAKUR

TOSS IT UP

AND TRUE LOVE WAITS
IN HAUNTED ATTICS
AND TRUE LOVE LIVES
ON LOLLIPOPS AND CRISPS
— RADIOHEAD

TRUE
LOVE
WAITS

TRUST YOUR PLACE IN TIME THOUGH YOU HAVE WON AND LOST
HOW VERY MUCH LIKE ME YOU ARE
WHEN YOU COME TO ME
TRULY, TRULY TRUST YOUR HEART
— THE KINKS

TRUST
YOUR
HEART

WELL I TRIPPED, I FELL DOWN NAKED
WELL I SCRATCHED MY KNEES, THEY BLED
SEW UP MY EYES, NEED NO MORE
IN OUR GAME THERE IS NO SCORE
— BILLY TALENT

TRY HONESTY

TRY TO HOLD ON, TO THIS HEART ALIVE
TRY TO HOLD ON, TO THIS LOVE ALOUD
TRY TO HOLD ON AND WE ARE STILL ALIVE
TRY TO HOLD ON AND WE HAVE SURVIVED
— SMASHING PUMPKINS

TRY, TRY, TRY

WE MUST BELIEVE IN THINGS WE CANNOT SEE
EVERYTHING'S ALRIGHT WITH ME
TURN THE LIGHTS DOWN
THE LIGHTS ARE TOO STRONG
— A-HA

TURN THE LIGHTS DOWN

HERE I AM
ON THE ROAD AGAIN
THERE I AM
UP ON THE STAGE
HERE I GO
PLAYIN' STAR AGAIN
THERE I GO
TURN THE PAGE
— BOB SEGER

TURN THE PAGE

THERE IS A SEASON - TURN, TURN, TURN
AND A TIME FOR EVERY PURPOSE UNDER HEAVEN
— THE BYRDS

TURN! TURN! TURN! (TO EVERYTHING THERE'S A SEASON)

WELL, SHAKE IT UP, BABY, NOW
TWIST AND SHOUT
C'MON, C'MON, C'MON, C'MON, BABY, NOW
COME ON AND WORK IT ON OUT
— THE ISLEY BROTHERS

TWIST AND SHOUT

U CAN'T TOUCH THIS
LOOK MAN U CAN'T TOUCH THIS
YOU'LL PROBABLY GET HYPED BOY
'CAUSE YOU KNOW YOU CAN'T U CAN'T TOUCH THIS
— MC HAMMER

U
CAN'T
TOUCH
THIS

IF I COULD BE YOU, IF YOU COULD BE ME
FOR JUST ONE HOUR, IF WE COULD FIND A WAY
TO GET INSIDE EACH OTHER'S MIND
IF YOU COULD SEE YOU THROUGH MY EYES
— JOE SOUTH

WALK A MILE IN MY SHOES

WALK LIKE A MAN, TALK LIKE A MAN
WALK LIKE A MAN MY SON
NO WOMAN'S WORTH CRAWLIN' ON THE EARTH
SO WALK LIKE A MAN, MY SON
— FOUR SEASONS

WALK LIKE A MAN

SLIDE YOUR FEET UP THE STREET BEND YOUR BACK
SHIFT YOUR ARM THEN YOU PULL IT BACK
LIFE'S HARD YOU KNOW
SO STRIKE A POSE ON A CADILLAC
— THE BANGLES

WALK LIKE AN EGYPTIAN

HOLLY CAME FROM MIAMI, FLA
HITCHHIKED HER WAY ACROSS THE USA
PLUCKED HER EYEBROWS ON THE WAY
SHAVED HER LEG AND THEN HE WAS SHE - SHE SAID:
"HEY BABE, TAKE A WALK ON THE WILD SIDE"
— LOU REED

WALK ON THE WILD SIDE

EVERYBODY'S TALKIN' 'BOUT A NEW WAY OF WALKIN'
DO YOU WANT TO LOSE YOUR MIND?
WALK RIGHT IN, SIT RIGHT DOWN
DADDY, LET YOUR MIND ROLL ON
— THE ROOFTOP SINGERS

WATCH WHAT YOU'RE SAYING
SOMEONE'S GONNA HEAR EXACTLY WHAT YOU SAID
SOON YOU'LL BE PAYING
— GURU

WHAT GOES AROUND, GOES AROUND, GOES AROUND
COMES ALL THE WAY BACK AROUND
— JUSTIN TIMBERLAKE

WHAT GOES AROUND COMES AROUND

WHAT THE WORLD NEEDS NOW IS LOVE, SWEET LOVE
NO, NOT JUST FOR SOME BUT FOR EVERYONE
— JACKIE DE SHANNOM

WHAT THE WORLD NEEDS NOW IS LOVE

THE MORE I LIVE
THE MORE I KNOW
WHAT'S SIMPLE IS TRUE
— JEWEL

WHAT'S SIMPLE IS TRUE

WHEN A PROBLEM COMES ALONG
YOU MUST WHIP IT
BEFORE THE CREAM SITS OUT TOO LONG
YOU MUST WHIP IT
— DEVO

WHIP IT

JUST WHISTLE WHILE YOU WORK
AND CHEERFULLY TOGETHER WE CAN TIDY UP THE PLACE
SO HUM A MERRY TUNE
IT WON'T TAKE LONG WHEN THERE'S A SONG
TO HELP YOU SET THE PACE
— SNOWWHITE & THE SEVEN DWARFS

WHISTLE WHILE YOU WORK

```
YOU ALWAYS HURT THE ONE YOU LOVE
THE ONE YOU SHOULDN'T HURT AT ALL
YOU ALWAYS TAKE THE SWEETEST ROSE
AND CRUSH IT TILL THE PETALS FALL
— MILLS BROTHERS
```

YOU ALWAYS HURT THE ONE YOU LOVE

YOU CAN GET IT IF YOU REALLY WANT
BUT YOU MUST TRY, TRY AND TRY, TRY AND TRY
YOU'LL SUCCEED AT LAST
— DESMOND DEKKER

YOU CAN
GET IT
IF YOU
REALLY
WANT

```
BABY, TAKE OFF YOUR COAT ... (REAL SLOW)
BABY, TAKE OFF YOUR SHOES ... (HERE, I'LL TAKE YOUR SHOES)
BABY, TAKE OFF YOUR DRESS
YES, YES, YES
— RANDY NEWMAN
```

YOU CAN LEAVE YOUR HAT ON

YOU CAN'T ALWAYS GET WHAT YOU WANT
BUT IF YOU TRY SOMETIMES WELL YOU MIGHT FIND
YOU GET WHAT YOU NEED
— THE ROLLING STONES

YOU CAN'T ALWAYS GET WHAT YOU WANT

YOU CAN'T BLAME IT ON ANYBODY
SOME THINGS THEY DON'T LAST
— PHOENIX

(YOU CAN'T BLAME IT ON) ANYBODY

YOU CAN'T HURRY LOVE
NO YOU JUST HAVE TO WAIT
SHE SAID LOVE DON'T COME EASY
IT'S A GAME OF GIVE AND TAKE
— THE SUPREMES

YOU CAN'T HURRY LOVE

```
IT DOESN'T PAY TO TRY
ALL THE SMART BOYS KNOW WHY
IT DOESN'T MEAN, I DIDN'T TRY
I JUST NEVER KNOW, WHY
- GUNS'N'ROSES
```

YOU CAN'T PUT YOUR ARMS AROUND A MEMORY

YOU CAN'T ROLLER SKATE IN A BUFFALO HERD
BUT YOU CAN BE HAPPY IF YOU'VE A MIND TO
— ROGER MILLER

YOU CAN'T ROLLER SKATE IN A BUFFALO HERD

BUT I BELIEVE SO STRONGLY IN YOU & I
CAN'T SOMEBODY ANSWER ME THE QUESTION WHY
YOU DON'T MISS YOUR WATER 'TIL THE WELL RUNS DRY
— CRAIG DAVID

YOU DON'T MISS YOUR WATER ('TIL THE WELL RUNS DRY)

DON'T GIVE UP
YOU'VE GOT A REASON TO LIVE
CAN'T FORGET
WE ONLY GET WHAT WE GIVE
— NEW RADICALS

YOU GET WHAT YOU GIVE

ANYTHING YOU WANT - YOU GOT IT
ANYTHING YOU NEED - YOU GOT IT
ANYTHING AT ALL - YOU GOT IT, BABY
— ROY ORBISON

YOU
GOT
IT

I, RECOMMEND BITING OFF MORE THAN YOU CAN CHEW TO ANYONE
I CERTAINLY DO
I, RECOMMEND STICKING YOUR FOOT IN YOUR MOUTH AT ANY TIME
FEEL FREE
— ALANIS MORISSETTE

YOU LEARN

YOU MAKE IT EASY TO WATCH THE WORLD WITH LOVE
YOU MAKE IT EASY TO LET THE PAST BE DONE
YOU MAKE IT EASY
— AIR

YOU MAKE IT EASY

WHEN SOMEBODY REACHES FOR YOUR HEART
OPEN UP AND LET THEM THROUGH
'COZ EVERYBODY NEEDS SOMEONE AROUND
THINGS CAN TUMBLE DOWN ON YOU
— RANDY CRAWFORD

YOU
MIGHT
NEED
SOMEBODY

YOU ONLY LIVE TWICE OR SO IT SEEMS
ONE LIFE FOR YOURSELF AND ONE FOR YOUR DREAMS
YOU DRIFT THROUGH THE YEARS AND LIFE SEEMS TAME
TILL ONE DREAM APPEARS AND LOVE IS ITS NAME
— NANCY SINATRA

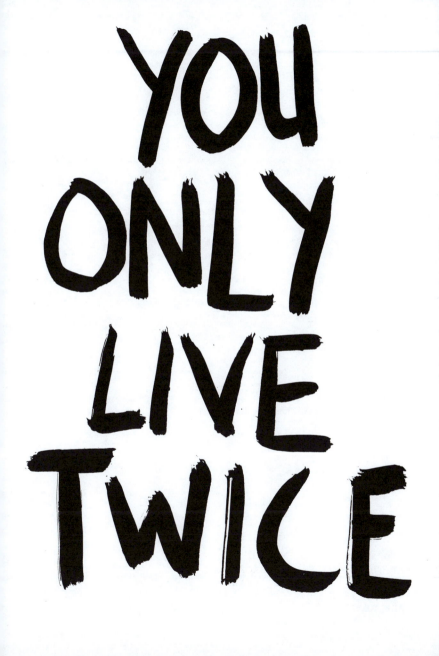

WHAT YOU DOIN' IN THE BACK AAH?
YOU SHOULD BE DANCING, YEAH
DANCING, YEAH
— BEE GEES

YOU SHOULD BE DANCING

IF THIS DOESN'T CURE YOU IT'LL KILL
BUT I KNOW IT'S GOING TO GIVE YOU A THRILL
AND NOW I'VE COME ACROSS DON'T COMPLAIN ABOUT THE COST
YOU SHOULDN'T CALL THE DOCTOR
IF YOU CAN'T AFFORD THE BILLS
— DR. FEELGOOD

492

YOU SHOULDN'T CALL THE DOCTOR (IF YOU CAN'T AFFORD THE BILLS)

A BIG BLABBERMOUTH, THAT'S WHAT YOU ARE
IF YOU WERE A TALK SHOW HOST, YOU'D BE A STAR
I SAID YOUR MOUTH IS BIG, SIZE EXTRA LARGE
AND WHEN YOU OPEN IT, IT'S LIKE MY GARAGE
— RUN-DMC

YOU
TALK
TOO
MUCH

DRIVE ME INSANE, TROUBLE IS GONNA COME TO YOU
ONE OF THESE DAYS AND IT WON'T BE LONG
YOU'LL LOOK FOR ME BUT BABY, I'LL BE GONE
THIS IS ALL I GOTTA SAY TO YOU WOMAN:
YOUR TIME IS GONNA COME
— LED ZEPPELIN

YOUR
TIME
IS
GONNA
COME

WALK ON! WALK ON! WITH HOPE IN YOUR HEART
AND YOU'LL NEVER WALK ALONE
— GERRY & THE PACEMAKERS

YOU'LL NEVER WALK ALONE

YOU MAY BE KING, YOU MAY POSSESS THE WORLD
AND IT'S GOLD, BUT GOLD WON'T BRING YOU
HAPPINESS WHEN YOU'RE GROWING OLD
— DEAN MARTIN

YOU'RE
NOBODY
'TIL
SOMEBODY
LOVES YOU

YOU'RE SO VAIN
YOU PROBABLY THINK THIS SONG IS ABOUT YOU
— CARLY SIMON

YOU'RE SO VAIN

WINTER, SPRING, SUMMER OR FALL
ALL YOU HAVE TO DO IS CALL
AND I'LL BE THERE
AIN'T IT GOOD TO KNOW THAT YOU'VE GOT A FRIEND
— CAROLE KING

YOU'VE GOT A FRIEND

HOW COULD SHE SAY TO ME
LOVE WILL FIND A WAY
GATHER ROUND ALL YOU CLOWNS
LET ME HEAR YOU SAY
HEY, YOU'VE GOT TO HIDE YOUR LOVE AWAY
— THE BEATLES

YOU'VE GOT TO HIDE YOUR LOVE AWAY

ARTIST INDEX

MARCUS KRAFT IS A GRAPHIC
DESIGNER AND ART DIRECTOR
BASED IN ZURICH, SWITZERLAND.
FROM HIS STUDIO, HE REAL-
IZES COMMISSIONED PROJECTS
FOR RENOWN CLIENTS AS
WELL AS SELF-INITIATED
PROJECTS. HIS FOCUS IS ON
ELABORATE DESIGN CONCEPTS,
EDITORIAL PROJECTS AND
TYPOGRAPHICAL QUALITY. HE
HAS BEEN AWARDED SEVERAL
INTERNATIONAL PRIZES FOR HIS
WORK. IN HIS SPARE TIME,
HE PLAYS THE DRUMS IN A ROCK
BAND.

WWW.MARCUSKRAFT.NET